The Warrior's Legend

Book 1

An Unofficial Minecraft Series

By Mr. Crafty

A special thanks to Zander, Caleb, David, and Lawrence.

Special thanks to Rafael Ibarra, riding off to The End on his skeleton horse.

Contents

Chapter 1: The Warriors

"Patience is a virtue. No matter how strong the temptation, to act without fully assessing the situation is to ensure your defeat"
- The Warrior's Code

The night was quiet and still. The moon shone brightly across the land, illuminating everything in an eerie blue haze, its reflection slowly rippling on the surface of the lake. A lone figure stood silhouetted against the flickering torchlight. Across the lake, a massive stone wall protected his village, and the torches on its parapets glowed orange behind him. Before him lay a dark, sprawling forest hiding any number of night creatures. He stood ready for anything but saw nothing.

"How much longer, Dulan?" he muttered under his breath. "Not much, just keep still until we give the signal," a nearby sweet berry bush whispered back.

Anyone else in his shoes would have been terrified, but Xander was bored out of his mind.

"I just don't understand why I still have to be the bait. You know I'm better than this," Xander hissed back towards the bush.

"You know our traditions. Now stay silent, lest you draw unnecessary attention," the shrub snapped back.

Xander wasn't just tired of being the bait. He was tired of the childish games he was forced to endure, the way the elders looked down on him, the humiliating chores he was made to do day in and day out. Xander was done being a child. He wanted to prove himself as an adult and move on with his life.

Slowly, from the nearby gathering of trees ahead, a lone zombie shuffled out of the darkness and made its way towards Xander, who noticed it but did not flinch. As it drew closer, another two came out, then six, soon more than a dozen were headed his way.

Finally, he thought to himself, *a little action to spice up the night.*

"Wait, something's not right," the bush said, noticeably louder than a whisper. "I think we need to regroup –"
Xander ignored the bush and pulled out his sword, the moonlight glinting off its iron tip as he let out his warrior cry.

"Xander! I said stand down!"

But it was too late.

TWIP

An arrow came flying from the heart of the dark forest. The sweet berry bush jostled hard and knocked Xander off his balance, causing the arrow meant for his heart to merely slice past his cheek and across his eye. Xander spun around and dropped his sword, clutching his bleeding face with both hands.

TWIP TWIP TWIP

Three more arrows flew from the darkness.

The bush let out a roar ten times as vicious as Xander's as a burly bear of a man jumped out of it and tackled Xander, taking in his own back the arrows meant for the boy. He dropped his giant axe as he collapsed on top of Xander, alive, but barely. Xander was pinned to the ground, his sword just out of reach as the zombies grew closer and the sound of the skeletons' arrows cut through the night.

"DULAN!" A woman's voice screamed out in horror. Suddenly, two more warriors rode in on horses from either side of the young would-be warrior, each pulling along a horse with no rider.

They jumped off their horses and worked together to lift the large man off Xander and onto the back of a horse. The horse's owner whispered something into the animal's ear and patted it on the backside, sending it off into the night. Xander reached his hand out to be helped up but the warriors ignored him, instead, turning to face the oncoming horde.

The two warriors stood side by side, the tall and slender man with a crossbow was named Asher, and the shorter blonde woman wielding a solid black netherite sword was Persephone. The duo stood motionless, surveying the battlefield. For them, time moved in slow motion. They whispered a plan to one another, so in sync, they seemed to finish each other's sentences. Only once was Xander even acknowledged when Persephone shot a disgusted look over her shoulder. Xander was physically, relatively unharmed, but his ego needed a medic. He stood up and looked past the two, trying to survey the battlefield for himself. It was time to tap into his warrior vision.

He had been honing this unique skill his entire life, but never on anything more than a few cattle, or one chained up zombie now and then. This was the first time he had ever used it in the heat of an actual battle. He closed his eyes and focused his mind. He took a deep breath and his eyes flashed open, everything in front of him now clear and sharp beyond description.

His view of the world narrowed as his full focus rested on the oncoming horde.

He saw the zombies as if they were in broad daylight, each one a shadow of its former, living self. But it was so much more than seeing. In this brief moment, he knew them. His advanced training kicking in, he noticed things he never would have before. One of the zombies had a limp, worse than the others. *This one must have fallen from a great height. If I could take out the leg in a low sweeping motion, I could leave it crumpled on the ground and could then focus on the others.*

Two zombies walked close to each other. Too close. These creatures were not pack animals and didn't tend to acknowledge each other's existence, let alone travel any sort of distance in this position. He homed in on them. *They are chained together at the leg. Perhaps they used to be prisoners.* He made a mental note not to run between them. He could trip on the hard-to-spot chain. He focused on the crowd again, surveying each reanimated corpse one by one. But his focus wavered. He lost sight of the important details and became overloaded by all the sensory information. The chorus of moans filled his ears, their sagging green skin and broken yellow teeth became a collage of horror. Lines blurred together as the wind's gentle caress brought with it the putrid smell of rot. He became light-headed and began to falter. He couldn't turn it off. His senses kept taking in more and more information and he had no way to process it.

The zombies didn't stop, and they didn't hesitate. They only came closer.

The three remaining horses were beyond spooked. This was unlike them, Xander noted. *They are trained just as much, if not more than we are to stay calm in the heat of battle.* Xander decided to block them out as he closed his eyes and took a deep breath once more, hoping to recenter himself. Instead of turning off his warrior's senses, he doubled down and blocked out every distraction, focusing instead on what was beyond the horde, where a far more pressing threat lay hidden.

He opened his eyes and stared beyond the undead, deep into the forest, the black shadows moving amongst the trees began to brighten and he could see each skeleton hiding while reloading or stepping out from their cover to aim. Are the monsters coordinating an attack? *No, that's impossible... Right?*

A blur passed before Xander's eyes and he immediately snapped out of focus, seeing the world normally once more. That blur had been Persephone. She surveyed the battlefield in a fraction of the time it took Xander and was off to bring her plan to fruition. She ran into the horde, zigzagging around the first few ghouls. She forward-rolled past another, the one with the limp, and hit its leg with her sword, sending the zombie tumbling, before getting back up.

As Xander stared awestruck, Asher stood his ground before him, picking off the zombies Persephone skipped with his crossbow. If he was scared or panicked, he certainly didn't show it. He appeared so calm it could almost have been mistaken for boredom. Without exchanging a word, Persephone and Asher performed their well-choreographed dance of destruction. Every zombie she passed he took down within seconds. He never missed. The sounds of his shooting and reloading were so precise they sounded automated. Persephone jumped impossibly high into the air and landed gracefully on the head of a zombie, effortlessly cutting a skeleton's arrow out of the air. She leapt onto the next zombie head and repeated the same defensive strikes as Asher sent a well-placed crossbow bolt into the head of the creature she had just departed. To see them in action was equal parts amazing and repulsive.

Not wanting to sit idly by and miss out on his chance for glory, Xander rallied himself to jump into the fray. He took one step forward to run into the field and was immediately snagged and tripped, landing flat on his face. *Was it a root or some small rock maybe?* He turned around and, horrified, saw the real reason the horses were bucking and whinnying. The shore of the lake he had foolishly kept his back to was covered in waterlogged undead slowly pulling themselves from the inky depths. The one that had its grip on Xander's ankle stared deep into his eyes. The milky white of its eyes invited Xander to spend an eternity in the cold dark waters with it. Its broken nails pressed into his leg, threatening to break the skin at any moment. Its mouth opened to let out a moan, but all that came out was a deep, bubbly gurgle as water and seaweed poured out.

Xander, well-trained warrior that he was, screamed like he'd never screamed before. All semblance of bravery he had was now out the window. He joined the horses in a panicked whinny.

Asher spun around and grabbed Dulan's fallen ax off the ground. Not used to the weight of the weapon, he grunted as he brought the blade down hard on the drowned's wrist. Xander then attempted to kick the severed hand off, but because of the creature's death grip, it took multiple tries. Once the hand lay on the shore twitching, Xander scurried backward as the maimed creature ignored the wound and dragged itself forward with its oozing stump and remaining hand.

The excitement proved to be too much for the horses who were now rearing back and kicking blindly. The startled animals were in full panic mode. Xander tried to calm one down and was kicked squarely in the chest and knocked to the ground. The horse spun around and saw that the zombies were now growing closer since Asher's attention was elsewhere. The horse backed away from the zombies and straight into the arms of the drowned. Xander, lying on the ground trying to catch his breath, shielded his eyes but could do nothing to block out the screams. Suddenly, he was lifted into the air and he opened his eyes to see Asher hoisting him onto a horse.

He started to climb up behind Xander when suddenly a crawling drowned sunk its sharp, moss-covered teeth into his leg. He let out a yell and tried to shake the creature off, but it was too late. The slowly approaching zombies had finally closed in. Asher hit Xander's horse and it took off without hesitation, still pulling the reins of the slain horse. The two sped along the edge of the lake as the two walls of death began to close in on either side, threatening to trap him in the middle. He never heard Asher scream, but he did hear Persephone.

She screamed Asher's name and started running back towards him. The skeletons in the woods took this opportunity to unleash a volley of arrows now that her back was to them.

TWIP TWIP TWIP TWIP TWIP TWIP TWIP TWIP

"PERSEPHONE!" Xander screamed out. She spun and cut through the arrows with her sword, but she wasn't fast enough to get all of them, and one found a new home buried in her shoulder.

She screamed as Xander turned the horse and galloped full speed towards her. The skeletons were still reloading by the time he reached her. She jumped onto her horse, snatched the reins from Xander, and headed towards Asher. But all she could see was a frenzied swarm of blue and green. And red. She averted her gaze and began riding on the path home as fast as her horse would take them.

The two raced back home in silence.

Chapter 2: The Kingdom

"Never let your guard down. For with us, the dead truly do not die, and betrayal can be as involuntary as breathing. Trust only in yourself and your instincts, all else is expendable."

- The Warrior's Code

The hidden town of Dragon Rock was truly a sight to be seen, though by design most would never have the opportunity to lay their eyes on it. It had been standing for centuries, but it hadn't always been hidden. It used to be the centerpiece of a sprawling kingdom, a very prosperous and successful kingdom, with an army as large as it was unbeatable. Therein lay the problem. Said to be tougher than diamond and braver than the fiercest wolf, the warriors of Dragon Rock were trained from birth. They surrendered to no one and followed their orders without question. For a while, the kingdom knew only peace. As word spread of these skilled soldiers, fewer and fewer souls tried to rob or harm others for fear of retaliation. They were the ultimate deterrent. Citizens from far and wide moved into the area just so they could be protected. But after a long stretch of peace, the soldiers grew bored. This boredom translated to restlessness and in many cases, this led to betrayal. Some members of the military felt that since they did the work, they should have the ability to rule. This led to a great schism, and ultimately, the defecting army was defeated and sent to the depths of the End. To prevent such an event from taking place ever again, changes were made to the warriors' time-honored traditions.

Dragon Rock slowly receded into the wilderness, letting the woods grow freely around it. The town did its best to wipe itself from the memories of the kingdom. Instead of chasing glory, they decided to work from the shadows to protect the citizens. This way, as people forgot about this group of protectors, the fame of the warriors would fade, and those who sought to join only for fame and glory would turn elsewhere.

No longer were soldiers trained from birth and taught to follow blindly, but rather given the option to train from a young age if they showed promise. This led to a coming of age ceremony in which each warrior was tested before being officially admitted into the army. This meant fewer soldiers, but loyalty that was tenfold. No longer forced into service, this was a choice each one made on their own. The soldiers were sent out on regular patrols to seek out dangers in order to prevent boredom and skill degradation. The most recent of these missions was to seek out the Ender Dragon and, if its existence were confirmed, to end it, lest it come to the surface and destroy the world. That was ten years ago, and while the dragon never appeared on the surface, neither did the team that was sent to hunt it down.

Queen Athena sat on her throne in the main hall of her castle, reminiscing about her kingdom's past, and specifically about that final mission all those years ago. Her advisor, Apophis, brought her back to the present with a polite, yet stern, clearing of the throat. She hadn't even realized her mind had wandered, and knew not how long she had been lost in thought.

"I apologize," she said to the pair of warriors bowing before her.

"N-no, my queen! We apologize to you! We can make our debriefing more...entertaining? If that is what you wish."

The queen chuckled. After all these years she still wasn't used to her subjects being so nervous around her.

"That won't be necessary," she said. "I'm just distracted. But please, continue. You have my undivided attention now."

The warrior nodded.

"Um, so anyway, we eliminated a few creepers around the mountainside. The concentration there seems to be heavier than normal. No signs of the witch, though we are looking into her possible involvement with the elevated creeper activity -"

BOOM!

The throne room doors burst open causing everyone in the main hall to jump, except for the interrupted warrior, who was more annoyed that he couldn't finish his mission summary than anything.

Two villagers struggled to carry Dulan into the throne room as a third ran ahead to a table, throwing everything off so they could carefully lay the injured man down. The village doctor ran into the room with his medical bag just seconds later.

"What is the meaning of this?" Apophis yelled, angrier at the break in protocol than the sight of the dying warrior before her.

"Stand down Apophis," the queen calmly told her advisor. She rose from her throne and walked towards the fallen man, careful to appear calm, and give no sign of the panic within. She gently placed her hand on Dulan's cheek.

"Dulan, I... What happened out there?"

Dulan slowly opened his eyes to look up at his queen, his breath was shallow and labored, it took him a moment to find the right words.

"Q- Queen Athena... It was... an ambush... Xander... he-AUGH!"

The doctor had begun to unstick one of the four arrows. Dulan gritted his teeth, his train of thought derailed for a moment.

The Queen felt faint. Xander's name was the last thing she wanted to hear, but she understood the reality of the situation and knew that he would have to be the first one brought up.

She felt weak in the knees and one of the men who brought in Dulan quickly brought a chair over for her to sit down and rest. Before she could, however, Apophis rushed over and shooed the man away, instead opting to adjust the chair ever so slightly in an attempt to take credit for the act.

The queen leaned forward, her face close to Dulan's. The doctor was deep in concentration, working to patch up the hole from the second removed arrow.

"Dulan is Xander… is he -"

"I don't know… for all I know… they are cleaning up now…
I was injured protecting Xander," he said through gritted
teeth.

Dulan squeezed his eyes shut and then relaxed as the doctor
finished pulling out the third arrow. The queen tried to get
more answers out of him, but it was pointless, he had passed
out from the pain.

The queen rose and started back towards her throne when
the doors of the room were thrown open once again. She
spun around to see Xander standing in the doorway. He was
out of breath and frozen in terror at the sight of Dulan's
limp body and the blood that trickled down as the doctor
worked tirelessly to patch up his wounds. Wounds that were
meant for Xander.

The hall had fallen silent. Xander slowly made his way
towards Dulan while Queen Athena approached Xander.
Two guards finished shutting the palace doors once more…
Only for them to be thrown open a third time!

"Oh for… Doesn't anyone knock anymore?" Apophis yelled in frustration.

It was Persephone, and she was livid. She stormed into the room with such fury that, had she been anyone else, she would have been tackled, shackled, and hauled off to the dungeon by now. But one does not simply arrest the captain of the army just for being angry. That was practically in the job description. Transfixed on Dulan, she stomped towards Xander, who was still moving slowly, and shoved him out of the way. He fell to the ground but instead of jumping back up, simply hung his head in shame. Everyone in the hall tensed up at once and looked towards the queen, who stared emotionless, taking in the scene before doing anything rash. She motioned for the guards to stop their approach on Persephone, and instead signaled for them to help Xander up. By the time he was up and dusted off, Queen Athena was next to him, she tried to comfort Xander, but he blew past her and left the main hall. She turned her attention to Persephone and Dulan. Persephone was trying to wake him but to no avail. She tried to hide her tears from the crowd that had gathered in the room but failed in this as well.

"Persephone, what happ –"

Persephone snapped her head at the queen and through gritted teeth said "You better hope Dulan pulls through. I will not lose my whole unit in one simple, preventable attack."

The queen raised her hand to her chest, trying to take in all this new information.

"Your whole… What happened to Asher?"

"He's dead." Persephone took a deep breath and fought to hold back her tears. "And if Dulan doesn't make it through the night, I'll see to it Xander joins them in the afterlife."

The Queen was shocked at this outburst, but she didn't let it show. She knew Persephone was a good person and a loyal soldier who was going through a lot. She had lost Asher, one of her unit, her best friend, and the brother to her fiancé who now lay bleeding out before her. Even so, that was no excuse to threaten the son of the queen.

Before she could offer any words of condolence, the doctor walked up to Athena, cleaning the blood off his hands with a rag.

"Just make sure you keep an eye on him. Make sure he stays hydrated and that he doesn't move and pop his stitches open… But he should make it. The arrows missed anything vital and I patched him up before he lost too much blood. He's a lucky man."

"He's not the lucky one," Persephone snapped as she looked up at the queen. "Your son is." And like that she was gone. The guards quickly scrambled to open the doors for her. After they closed the doors, they looked towards the queen for orders, but she too was gone. They looked at each other and shrugged.

Xander was on top of an old archer tower outside the city walls. He liked it up there. It wasn't used much these days, so it gave him the privacy he craved without his having to venture out to anywhere dangerous. He wasn't scared, mind you, but why put yourself into danger unnecessarily?

He was alone in the cool night air, looking over everyone in the village going about their evening. He was finally isolated enough to let go and cry when suddenly he heard footsteps behind him. He assumed it was Persephone coming to hurt him for his grave mistake. He tensed up but made no effort to defend himself. He deserved whatever was coming. Instead of a cold blade, however, he felt his mother's warm voice.

"I know you've been through a lot, my son, but I need to know what happened out there."

"My queen," he began but was interrupted.

"I'm not here as your monarch, but as your mother, and I don't expect an official report. I'm just worried about my son."

And just like that he wasn't a soldier, wasn't a warrior in training anymore. He felt like a scared little kid. He embraced his mom and began sobbing uncontrollably. His tears flowed freely and with them came the story of what just happened. He told her about his impatience, his recklessness, how Dulan took the arrows for him, and how Asher's last act on this earth had been to save him. He told her about the long, silent ride back. He bared his soul to her, and when he was done, he heard only silence. He pulled away from her, wiping his eyes to get a good look at her and to his surprise found she was holding back tears herself.

"If it's any consolation, Dulan will make it through the night. As for Asher...we'll send someone out in the morning to see if there is anything left to recover, then we'll have a proper remembrance ceremony."

Her voice was hollow and trembling, and she was staring out into nothing.

"Persephone is understandably devastated right now," she continued. Xander visibly flinched at the mention of her name.

"So, we may have to find you a different unit. I can send her out to one of our remote barracks until her rage cools down. At the very least we'll postpone your final test."

Xander couldn't believe what he was hearing. Surely, he had misheard her. After causing the damage he had, how could he possibly be allowed to continue with his training? Anyone else would have been cast out of the village, if not executed.

He couldn't let this happen. It wasn't fair to anyone.

"Mother, I… I can't. I need to be punished. I can't be allowed to -"

"You dare speak out against your queen?"

Just like that, she changed roles again. There would be no arguing with her. She turned and left. She had much to do today.

Xander tossed and turned all night but sleep evaded him. Every time he closed his eyes, he saw the incident from earlier, repeating, over and over. He stared at the ceiling of his room hearing the screams of the horse and Asher echo through the night until he was brought to attention by a very real scream just a few rooms away.

He ran out into the hall to see one of the servant girls stumble backward out of the room Dulan was recovering in. She screamed for help and, without hesitation, Xander ran over to help her up. He looked in the direction she was pointing and immediately wished he were dreaming. Standing in the room, slowly making his way towards the two of them was Dulan, or what used to be Dulan.

He was dead, but on his feet, green and moaning. The girl screamed again even louder but Xander could not stop staring. He couldn't - or didn't want to - believe what he was seeing. The girl broke away from his shocked grip and ran down the halls screaming even louder, trying to get anyone else to come to her rescue as Xander started walking towards the remains of his friend. His slow pace matched the ghoul's.

This can't be happening.

He was now in the doorway, still transfixed while the sound of footsteps came pounding down the hallway. He was within arms-reach of the undead Dulan when he heard someone shout, "Get down my lord!" and was tackled to the ground. He lay there stunned and watched the guards end the unlife of his friend. Dulan's body crumpled next to him on the floor.

The queen stepped into the room, quickly surveyed what had happened, and turned to the guards.

"I need you two positioned outside of Persephone's house. Don't let her see you, but don't let anyone in either. I don't want her to find out about this until I break it to her personally in the morning."

And just like that, everyone left. Xander lay alone on the floor next to the slain zombie for the remainder of the night.

Chapter 3: The Departure

"And when the queen feels they are truly ready, the sons and daughters of Dragon Rock will venture into the depths of the unknown and claim a warrior's trophy before the depths can claim the same from them."
- The Warrior's Code

One year later.

Xander was out of bed and pacing his room long before the sun had risen. This was the day he'd been waiting for his whole life, but instead of excitement, all he felt was shame and despair.

He should have been dead, in prison, or living in the woods for what happened a year ago, but here he was, comfortably living in the second largest bedroom in the castle. He should have been starved and beaten, but instead, he was fed and pampered. At the very least, he should not have been allowed to complete the ritual and become a full-fledged warrior, for the reasons stated above as well as the fact that he was now one year too old. But his mother was the queen, and exceptions were made, and now his dreams were coming true. He should have been excited, but he hated every part of it.

As soon as the sun came up, horns blared a melody not heard for many years. The song alerted the village that one of their own was going to become one of their elite protectors or die trying. There was no avoiding this. It was his time.

As he left his room, he caught his reflection in the mirror. He looked noticeably older than he did a year ago. His cheeks were a bit more gaunt and dark circles had found permanent residence under his eyes. But the main difference was the large scar he now had across his cheek and over his eye. The apothecary had said he could fix it shortly after the injury happened, but he had refused, choosing instead to wear it as a daily reminder of his failure.

He stepped out of the palace to the thunderous roar of applause, everyone in the town was there cheering and screaming for him. Many of the townsfolk felt like he was their own child. Xander was never one for pomp and circumstance; he had at one point or another personally helped each and every one of these people before deciding to dedicate his life to protecting them all. They cheered and offered compliments and gifts, all of which he ignored or refused. Nothing they could give him could fill the emptiness he felt inside.

He walked down the long red carpet, lined with villagers on either side, towards his mother who was seated at the end. He felt worse than he ever had before. Because of him, two of their own were dead and many of their sacred traditions had been broken, yet here they stood, cheering him on as if nothing had happened at all. It filled him with disgust.

Everyone treated him like nothing had happened, except, of course, *her.*

His eyes landed on Persephone, whom he had hardly seen since the incident. This was by design, of course. The queen had sent her on all types of missions and outings, anything to keep her away from Xander. Persephone didn't bother to hide her scowl of discontent and that suited him just fine. It was refreshing, the honesty of it. Her look matched the one he gave himself every morning in the mirror. If he weren't so sure she would beat him for it, he would have smiled knowing that someone else saw him the way he saw himself. To Xander's dismay, the cancelation of the ceremony was never even considered. He had learned to accept that and found some comfort in the fact that whether he earned his place among the warriors or fell in the attempt, this horrible feeling he lived with would be over either way.

He made it to the end of the red carpet and knelt before his mother, the queen. She stood, and the crowd quieted as she began her speech.

"Today is the day Xander will venture into the Nether to complete his rite of passage and become a true warrior. As is tradition, he will go down into the darkness of the Nether and return with a wither skull, or he won't return at all. Should he prove successful, he will be one of our chosen few protectors; our elite, our proud, our brave defenders."

He could feel Persephone staring daggers into the back of his neck. The queen continued but Xander's mind was elsewhere. He didn't care to hear about the history of the kingdom, the schism, the civil war, and the changes made.

He also didn't care to hear about the last major mission, the unsuccessful attempt to slay the Ender Dragon led by none other than his father. He wanted more than anything to be past this part.

He looked around the crowd at the excited, smiling faces. Did anyone know what really happened the day Asher died? How many details had been left out or altered to protect their opinion of him? How many thought the two soldiers perished on account of their own mistakes, adding insult to injury? *If that was true, no wonder Persephone seems to hate me even more after all this time.*

"...as we wish Xander all the luck in the world."

Finally, she was done, now she would ask him to rise and he could be on his way. Only, she didn't. She broke tradition again and continued.

"As you all know, I didn't want this to continue. This ceremony was never to take place under these circumstances."
Was Xander hearing this right?

"After the terrible incident last year, after losing two of our own, how could any mother want this for her son?"

Xander cringed at the mention of the incident and could only imagine Persephone's reaction.

"Xander was to be removed from the military and given diplomatic duties."

He swallowed hard in surprise. This was news to him.

"But every single one you came to me begging and pleading to let young Xander continue his training, to make his dream come true and to allow him to serve. Many rules have been bent and broken, but only at your behest. Today, Xander begins his final test because of each and every one of you. Had even one of you had reservations about this, I wouldn't have considered it, but miraculously the decision was unanimous."

Xander couldn't help himself, he looked up at Persephone who was staring straight ahead. Did she really give the go-ahead for this?

"So, rise, Xander. And make the kingdom who fought so hard for you proud."

He stood up to even louder thunderous applause and he looked around at everyone cheering and chanting his name. A tear formed in his eye, the first in a long time that he wasn't ashamed of, and a small smile spread across his face as fireworks burst in the sky.

Maybe he didn't know everything after all.

The people of the town were sending him off in a grand fashion. He had never seen anything like it. Since the warriors had disappeared into the End, there hadn't been much cause for celebration. This was the first time everyone in the town had come together in agreement like this, at least, as far as Xander could remember. He was only a child when he saw his father leave.

Xander looked around at everyone with renewed awe and confidence as the fireworks went off. He waved and tried to thank the crowd but couldn't be heard over the cheering. Instead, he turned on his heel and headed for the stables with a renewed pep in his step.

As soon as he got to the stables a saddle was thrown at him, hard. He caught it and started to walk towards a horse he'd never seen before.

This must have replaced one of the -
"Come on if you're coming," Persephone snapped as she mounted a horse of her own.

She began stroking the horse's mane.

"Shh, calm Dulan, the mean man can't hurt you. I won't let him."

Xander stood in stunned silence.

"Well, what are you waiting for? Saddle up Asher and we'll be on our way."

It was like a knife being twisted in his gut. He put the saddle on Asher and climbed on.

"So… you named the horses after them."

Her horse neighed as it popped up on its hind legs.

"You should see what I named after you."

And she was off.

They rode in silence to a cave. The awkwardness reminded Xander of the ride back to town the night Asher died. The queen arrived at the cave soon after with her guards and Apophis, and formally wished Xander good luck. She then pulled him in for a hug to wish him luck personally.

"Wherever your father is, just know he is so very proud of you, my son. I look forward to your return," she whispered in his ear before handing him a red torch and sending him into the cave.

The cave was dark and foreboding, but no different from any other cave at first glance, at least physically. Xander couldn't be sure if it were only in his head, or if his sensitive warrior instincts were picking up on something, but the air felt heavy and important. He was nervous, yet somehow calm at the same time. Clueless as to what he was to be doing, while confident he would know when the time came. *This must be what it's like to be a warrior.* The feeling was intoxicating and almost made him forget about his hesitation and anxiety. As he walked deeper into the cave, the natural light dimmed, casting Xander and his surroundings in the eerie red light from his torch. Once he was deep enough that he could hardly see the entrance, he found a pedestal made from gold and decorated with diamonds and emeralds. It was the most ornate and beautiful work of art he had ever seen, and he grew up in the royal palace. He walked up to it and carefully but firmly placed the red torch in a hole carved into the top. It clicked into place and sank in with a whirring noise, red now shining through the ornate carvings and revealing youthful figures stepping into a square hole. The cave entrance slammed shut and a tunnel in the rock opened before him.

Chapter 4: The Cave

"A true warrior trusts in the warrior's intuition. For individual senses can be tricked and misled, but a warrior learns to see beyond that which is presented to them."
- The Warrior's Code

Xander squinted to adjust to the eerie but slowly becoming familiar red light flooding in from the newfound tunnel. Once he was used to it, he examined the walls around him and found a small switch. He wasn't sure about pressing it, but after further searching, he found no other option, so he pressed it and heard a click. Some mechanical noises whirred and clicked in rapid succession, coming from everywhere and nowhere at the same time. Suddenly, torches began lighting themselves all along the cave walls, showing him the cave room in its entirety and leading him further down the tunnel. It was much larger than he had anticipated. The sounds of the torches lighting continued long after the ones near him were lit.

Now that the cave was no longer pitch black, Xander saw the beauty of it.

It all felt so pure and natural. Even though he was far from the first person here, he couldn't help but feel like he was the one that discovered it. The stone had been worn away over time by nature, not a pickaxe. The stalactites and stalagmites were bigger than him, some even meeting in the middle. The air wasn't stale like he had expected. It was cool and clean, and it was quiet. This is what surprised him the most. He could hear his footsteps echo softly, and water dripping off in the distance, but other than that it was silent. This was the most peaceful place he had ever been.

As he walked, he noticed the walls were packed full of untouched resources. Veins of coal and iron to his left, and to his right the walls were lined with Redstone and Lapis. It was something he had never experienced before. Every cave he had been in before was for training or to clean out monsters, all of which had been long since stripped of their ore and natural beauty. His world had felt so industrialized, but not here. Xander got lost in the glory of the cave until he was interrupted by an all too familiar sound, a sound he had heard in his nightmares every night for the past year.

TWIP TWIP

Arrows flew past Xander's head as he ran for cover behind a low stone wall. He had no idea exactly where they were coming from, just that the shooter was somewhere in front of him.

"I can't believe I didn't see that coming," he mumbled to himself.

Xander unsheathed his sword and peeked around the corner. Two skeletons, each with their own bow, were looking in his direction, but they didn't see exactly where he had gone.

He decided to try and attract their attention. If he could at least lure one closer, he wouldn't have to run headfirst into two sets of deadly arrows. Back pressed against the stone wall he whistled and clanged his sword against the wall, hoping to make enough noise to keep their interest. It was working! The skeleton came closer and closer.

48

When it was just about in reach for Xander's fatal strike it stopped and turned its head directly to face him. Xander stared into its empty sockets and his heart skipped a beat. It stared back, unmoving. It didn't flinch or attempt to shoot him or anything. It just stared. Xander gulped. Should he risk attacking now? Before he could come to a decision, the skeleton continued past him for a few steps before it turned around and surveyed the part of the cave it had just come from. Are they actually blind after all? As if it could read his mind the skeleton locked eyes with Xander once more, then clanked its teeth together.

What is going –
"SSSSSSSSSSSS"

The unmistakable hiss of a creeper coming from the other side of the wall. He dove forward at the last second.

KABOOM!

The wall was obliterated. Only smoke, rubble, and a few bones scattered about remained. Xander let out a sigh of relief, his journey had almost ended before it began.

TWIP

If the smoke from the explosion and rubble wasn't obscuring the environment, the arrow would have met its mark. The miasma of smoke and dust was disrupted where the arrow had cut through, creating a perfect circle. Xander closed his eyes and focused on the sounds of the creaking bones and reloading bow. He held his sword over his head, the tip of the blade brushing against his back as he waited for one more sound to give him confirmation. He heard the string of the bow pulling back, bending the wood, its creak magnified to his hyper-focused senses. With all his strength he threw his sword towards the noise. It flew through the smoke, a high-speed spinning wheel of destruction. The skeleton realized where Xander was standing at the last second and shifted its aim. Xander was staring at the tip of the arrow but his sword flew true and stuck into the creature's skull, right between the sockets. The skeleton fell backward and its arrow hit the ceiling of the cave. A pile of rocks and debris came crashing down on top of him, burying his bones and Xander's sword for good.

Just my luck.

Xander wiped the sweat off his forehead. His whole body shaking, he sat down to take a breather. He looked around the cave just to make sure he was alone.

What happened a year ago, the ambush in the field, had all happened so fast it seemed like a fluke. But this right here, this was positive proof. The creatures were working together somehow.

Now all he had to do was figure out how, and why, and somehow survive his trial and make it all the way back to Dragon Rock to warn his people. All without a sword.

Great.

After a few minutes of rest, Xander finally got up and dusted himself off. He picked up a sturdy-looking bone and swung it around a few times to get a feel for it. Instead of keeping it, he tossed it over his shoulder, deciding it wasn't worth the attempt. He continued in the direction the skeletons had come from, continuing to take in the cave's natural beauty but never once letting down his guard. At least, not anymore. He was weaponless, but he wasn't defenseless. His wits and senses could get him through this mess. He just had to be careful not to let anything get the jump on him again.

He wandered through the cave, stopping at every fork and intersection to let his warrior senses show him the right way to go. The whole point of this part of the trial was to trust in your senses enough to find your way through unfamiliar territory. There wasn't supposed to be any combat. Were those monsters here because it had been so long since there was a trial? No, that didn't make sense. The caves were sealed off and maintained for this very reason. Whatever was going on Xander didn't like it.

After what seemed like hours of twisting and turning through the tunnels, he noticed an inscription on the wall. He was well versed in what to expect on his trial and knew he must be nearing the end of the cave if there were writing on the wall.

He had studied the ancient language, but this was a much older dialect than he was used to. He was unable to decipher it fluently, but he made out the gist of the passage. This was one of the oldest known versions of "The Warriors Code." This particular passage signified that his senses had proven true, and that he had successfully navigated the first part of the trial. There were a few sections in the middle he was lost on, but he picked it up again towards the end. He was to find another switch that would open another door that… The rest of the passage, the wall for that matter, was gone. The doors that were supposed to be sealed and hidden were open, busted, and broken. The redstone piston of one of them was repeatedly jutting out then retreating into the wall. He carefully walked past it, cautious not to get smashed, and stepped over the rubble. He now found himself in the room that housed the nether portal, its creepy, purple light shimmering and dancing in unison with its low, dull hum. This was expected, but still awe-inspiring. Unfortunately, the sight of this wonder of the world was diminished by something completely unexpected. Beside the portal were two dead iron golems.

These golems, in their living state, were there on the off chance any creature made it through the portal into this realm. These brutes were stationed here to throw it back through or take it out if need be. They were more than enough to handle anything that stumbled through. But now they were lying on the ground in pieces.

The coordinated attack theory was sounding more and more plausible. Against everything in his body telling him not to, Xander stepped up onto the obsidian and allowed himself to be swallowed by the purple.

Chapter 5: The Portal

"Purple is a noble color indeed. The pigments and dyes used to make it are desired by the warrior above all others. For who but a warrior could look into the great purple abyss and step through without hesitation?"
- *The Warrior's Code*

Xander's vision was purple, hazy, and blurred. Nothing made sense. Up was down and left was right. At one point he even thought his feet and his hands had switched places. He'd heard about traveling through the portal, but nothing, NOTHING could have prepared him for what it was actually like.

After twirling and swirling for what seemed like hours, but also seconds, the world started to put itself back together. Everything was finally still. He was queasy and dizzy but, now that he was on solid ground, he felt like he was going to be ok. He was stepping off the obsidian when he realized he was not going to be ok; there was nothing there.

He hugged the side of the portal, considering stepping back through the purple when all of a sudden it fizzled out. He was now suspended high in the air in an obsidian frame with no way out. Something must have destroyed the portal from the other side! Something had definitely done some damage here too. There was supposed to be a walkway here that led to a fortress.

This was supposed to be a test, not a *suicide mission*. From his narrow perch, he decided to take in his surroundings and try to figure out a way down.

He was in the biggest cavern that he had ever seen. Endless lava lay below him in what seemed like a sea of death. Waterfalls of molten fire poured from the ceiling, feeding the fiery ocean. Across the cavern, Xander spotted pig men everywhere. He had heard tales of how vicious they could be if one were to provoke them. Something else caught his attention in the distance. He couldn't quite make out what was happening, but he saw a tall, purple figure. Then, it zipped around to another place. It was moving so fast and teleporting so randomly that it was impossible to tell what *exactly* it was.

Bringing his attention back to his current situation he noticed some hard-looking red ground below him. He noted that a fall from this height would be survivable but definitely not comfortable. He was weighing his options when suddenly something white caught his eye. A large, flying puffy creature was slowly coming his way. It was large enough for him to jump onto. If he could land on it just right, he'd be able to guide it down to the ground. While drifting closer, this ghastly creature let out a scream that almost made Xander reconsider his whole plan. It was like an injured baby's cry combined with the howl of a wounded animal. He was not easily frightened but that noise shook him to the core. He ignored his gut. It was now or never. The creature was going to be directly under him… NOW! Xander threw caution and his body to the wind and jumped from his perch, hurtling towards the creature much faster than he anticipated. He braced himself for impact and hoped the creature wouldn't mind this too much.

It didn't.

Turns out they're incorporeal. Something Xander wished he had known before diving from the relative safety of the portal, through the creature and towards the unforgiving red floor.

He wasn't sure how long he was knocked out, or if he had actually been unconscious at all, but his head was pounding and the squishy, splashing sound very close to him was not improving his situation. A weird red blob with flaming eyes was flopping around like a fish out of water just inches from his face. He quickly sat up and made direct eye contact with the blob as it frantically flopped towards him. Xander stood up as the creature was about to touch him and gave it a swift kick, sending it hurtling towards a wall. It smacked into the wall with a splat and was no more. Xander turned around, but before he could walk away, he heard more splashing sounds.

He turned back to see two slightly smaller blobs where only one had been moments before. Being the quick learner he was and not having a proper weapon, Xander decided this wasn't worth his time and set off to truly start his quest. A fortress loomed in the distance. He was sure it was full of things waiting to kill him, but that beat being out in the open.

Right?

Chapter 6: The Ghast

"...and I saw the white figure floating, it's limbs a calming lullaby. One would almost let one's guard down, were it not for the screech it makes; like a wolf cub left to die in the cold."
- The Warrior's Code

Xander had known this journey would be hard, but he couldn't have imagined half of the things he had experienced so far. As he slowly made his way to the fortress, he couldn't help but think the entire world was against him. The most unsettling revelation of all was that everything he thought he knew was wrong. From the way the village really thought about him to how the creatures had been acting lately, it was like his whole worldview had been turned inside out.

And don't get me started on this test.

This journey was supposed to be more of a formality than anything, he'd done the training and combat tests and passed all his scholarly subjects. He had been told everything to expect along the way. The trial was more for show and ceremony and not actually meant to be this dangerous. But here he was, stranded in the Nether without a weapon, all his expectations shattered. This truly was a test to prove himself, a test of survival. He wondered what his dad would have done in this situation.

Based on his last mission, get killed, never come back, and leave his family alone to mourn and miss him.

Xander shook his head. That was bleak. Perhaps this place was affecting him more than he thought.

He had to focus and push through his test before he could become a warrior, like his father, and remain alive, unlike his father. He didn't want to put his mom through that again. He stopped and concentrated. The noises and smells of this place were making it hard for him to focus. He needed to bring back… something. He couldn't remember, but he was sure it had to do with the fortress. He marched onward, positive it would come back to him once he got there. Besides, there's a better chance of another portal being in there than out here.

His thoughts distracted him from the real dangers right in front of him.

Xander gasped for air as his left foot plunged into a large hole in the ground he had been too distracted to notice. His stomach dropped, and he threw himself backward, landing hard on his back. His life flashed before his eyes as he imagined plummeting into the endless hole. How could his senses have failed him so badly? Why was he allowing himself to get so distracted?

Xander stood and dusted himself off. Regaining his composure, he carefully stepped around the whole as he continued towards the fortress.

Determined to make it to the fortress before something else came out of nowhere to kill him, he sprinted towards the great red structure until he heard an otherworldly sound.

"Rrrreeeee!"

Xander turned around quickly. He had no idea where that sound came from. Could it be those blobs coming back for him? Or maybe a wither skeleton? After all, Xander had only heard tales of the creatures that dwell here, so he didn't know what sound belonged to which monster. The whole list of monsters that could be after him raced through his mind. His careful sprint turned into a full-on, mad dash to safety. Whatever this was, he doubted he could defeat it with his fists alone.

"Rrreeeeee!"

The young warrior had not felt terror like this since that fateful night a year ago. Xander couldn't possibly run any faster. He saw movement in the distance. White, dangling tentacles hovered, swaying gently.

Xander was so relieved he almost burst out laughing.

One of these? Ha! I can pass right through them, I thought that noise was something that could actually hurt me!

"*Rrreeeee!*"

BOOM!

Xander was knocked off his feet by a fireball from the mouth of the ghostly figure.

The sound of heavy boulders shifting made Xander immediately look upward as dislodged red rocks came crashing down from above. He had no time to react because the ghostly creature was charging up for another attack.

"Rrreeee!"

BOOM!

More blocks fell all around him. He scurried backward to avoid being crushed, and panic began to set in. A surge of adrenaline threatened to rob him of his rational thinking and throw him into a terrified panic, but suddenly something clicked, and he began to calm down. His training was kicking in. He took a deep breath.

Blocks continued to fall toward and around Xander, but to him, the blocks now seemed to be falling much more slowly. He let himself fall backward and curled into a backward somersault as a heavy rock slammed down right where he had just been. He thrust himself onto his feet and continued to walk backward as rocks narrowly missed him. He weaved left and right, stepping just out of the way before the rocks could land a deadly blow.

"Rrreeeee!"

BOOM!

He jumped into the air and grabbed a falling boulder. As soon as he landed, he braced himself, and the blast hit the rock dead on, destroying his stony shield and sending him flying backward. His body tensed as he fell to the ground. He expected to hit solid rock, but, to his surprise, he landed on something loose and… boney?

He jumped up and saw that he had landed on a skeleton archer who had come by to investigate all the noise. It looked just as startled as he did, but he managed to get up first.

"Rrreeeee!"

He bent down and ripped the bow from the hands of the confused monster. At least he tried to, but unfortunately, the skeleton's hands and arms came with it. He grabbed an arrow that had fallen out of the skeleton's quiver and readied his aim, which was very hard to do with the disembodied arms flailing about, smacking his head and face. He took another deep breath and focused, past the rocks, debris, angry bones. He waited for the perfect moment.

TWIP

The arrow soared through the air. It spun as it sped towards the ghast, narrowly missing rocks and debris, a one in a million shot.

BOOM!

The arrow hit its target – the fireball meant for Xander – and the creature was engulfed in the flames. It let out an unholy scream as it crashed into the lava where it slowly sank below the surface.

The chaos had stopped. The blocks were no longer falling to the ground. The monster had been defeated. Before he could take a well-deserved break, the ground below him started to move. Suddenly he remembered he was standing on an angry, armless skeleton and it was trying to stand up. He hopped off as the arm still holding onto the bow started aggressively wailing on him.

A solid hit across the jaw made him instinctively recoil in pain, dropping the bow. As if by magic, the bones found their home in the empty sockets of the monster. The skeleton now stood before him, rearmed in more ways than one. It aimed its bow at Xander's face. With limited options and nowhere to go, he grabbed onto the bow and threw his head back while raising the bow.

TWIP

The feather on the end of the arrow tickled his chin as it flew by. In a desperate struggle, Xander pulled the bow towards himself while kicking the skeleton in the chest, trying to get the bow back, but to no avail. The skeleton grabbed another arrow but instead of loading the bow, stabbed Xander in the hand. He let go in an instant and sent the grip of the bow slamming into the skeleton's sternum, knocking it off balance and into the lava. The bow and the monster were gone, but at least he was alive. He stood up and looked towards the fortress. As hard as it had been to get there, he could only imagine what waited for him beyond those walls.

Chapter 7: The Fortress

"The buildings of the other world are nothing like our own. The endless corridors are meant to trap lost spirits and confuse those not meant to be there. To explore the fortress is to tempt death herself"
– The Warrior's Code

Xander was finally at the fortress, and it loomed enormous over him. Surrounding the large red castle was a river of lava with only a narrow bridge allowing him to cross.

Xander took his first step onto the netherbrick bridge. It was firm, stable. With the way things had been going lately, he half expected it to crumble underneath him. So, this was a bit of good news. Everything that he had experienced in life had brought him to this point, and he couldn't have been more ready. A small smile spread across his face as he confidently walked up to the eerie fortress.

He crossed the bridge at a steady pace, testing the stability of each step before he put his full weight down. He didn't come this far to end up in the lava now. His slow approach only served to make the fortress seem more and more intimidating. It was so massive that when he was finally across the bridge, it was almost all he could see. He paused at the entrance, not scared, but cautious. A hot wind softly blew out of the fortress, almost as if it were alive and breathing onto him. He pushed the thought from his head and found his confidence again. He slowly crossed the threshold and was struck with awe. He found himself in a massive corridor leading who knew where that stretched on further than he could see. He got the feeling it was somehow bigger on the inside. But strangest of all, it was quiet, almost dead. Xander was expecting some sort of gathering of monsters, maybe a dark kingdom, or legions of zombies. Instead, he found nothing. It was as if this fortress had been reclaimed by the Nether itself and everything in it had left... or worse. This got him thinking. How was he supposed to find a wither skeleton if there was nothing here?

He closed his eyes and once more channeled his warrior sense, but even this yielded no results. Whether this meant there was truly nothing here, or that the Nether was starting to deafen his abilities, he didn't know, but he hoped it was the former. Since his warrior sense wasn't telling him anything new, all he could do was find his goal the old-fashioned way: a lot of exploring and more than a little luck.

After wandering corridors aimlessly for about an hour, Xander found a small, sheltered room and sat down to take a break. At this point, his frustration was overwhelming, and he wanted nothing more than to be back at home. Even if he came back a failure, doomed to the drudgery of politics and royal duties for the rest of his life, at least he would be home. But there was no turning back now. How would he even get back home? He was trapped in the Nether, and the only way out was forward.

Why does finding a wither skull have to be so hard? How did the previous warriors all do it? Are there even any left?

Xander's thoughts centered on self-doubt. He wondered what would happen if he returned home without a skull.

Or worse still, what if he never found an exit? Would he ever return home at all? He snapped out of it. This was not a time to be doubting himself.

He was from a warrior tribe, so he knew that he could not back down from any quest, no matter what he had to face. Xander gathered his strength and decided to continue looking.

Wandering through the long, wearying hallways, Xander finally stumbled upon something he hadn't run into yet. An everyday chest sat in the middle of the otherwise empty room. He slowly crept towards the chest and popped it open. All that was inside was paper. Out of all things, paper?

Why is there a random chest out here? Confused, but uninterested, Xander just left the paper in the box. It didn't seem to be a map or anything important, and it wasn't like he could use it as a weapon. Xander continued his journey through the fortress.

The layout of the hallways continued to confuse him. He wondered why all the bricks were the same color and had the exact same design. These meaningless thoughts were interrupted by a disgusting sound.

"Squeeeeee!"

It was such a low-pitched, grating noise after hours of silence that it sent chills running down Xander's spine. This wasn't a time to freeze in fear, especially with an unknown entity nearby. He quickly hid in the nearest room.

Thud. Thud. Thud.

He peeked around the corner and saw three monsters stomp past the room, their steps heavy and deliberate. Their skin was pink, their ears flopped down to their chins and they had horrible tusks and hooves.

"Pig men," he mumbled to himself.

This wasn't the monster he was looking for, and although he had learned in training that they were weak in combat, he was still outnumbered three to one with no weapon. On top of that, they were headed in the same direction as he was, down a long corridor that offered no cover should they decide to turn around. He looked around at his feet and found a small rock. If he could throw it down one of the branching hallways, he might be able to distract them long enough to run past. It was a longshot. If he couldn't make it far enough down the corridor, they would surely see him and give chase. Not to mention the possibility that more pig men may be lurking down the side hallways. But it was a risk he was going to have to take. He readied the stone, waiting for them to pass the hallway he was aiming for.

Steady...

Steady...

NOW!

He threw the stone as hard as he could, and it flew across the hallway into another room where it hit the wall with a loud clang!

Shoom, shoom, shoom...

BOOM!

An explosion rocked the room the rock had landed in, a huge chunk of wall now gone, a dark window into the depths of the Nether.

There is no way I threw the rock that hard, Xander thought to himself.

The pig men quickly turned around and ran towards the room. Xander thought that maybe this had been one of those ghost creatures he had encountered earlier. Regardless, it wasn't his problem. He should be thanking it. That explosion was a much better distraction than his rock. He wasted no time and started to make his way past the room but stopped at the entryway, distracted by the destruction. It was like a minecart wreck. He couldn't look away.

There was a giant hole in the wall. He could see the Nether clearly through it, but it was a side he hadn't seen before. He hadn't realized how high up he had climbed in the fortress, or how large a lake of lava could be. The pillars of light and the movement of creatures in the distance surprised him. He never realized how active and full of life it was down in the depths. This was something he hadn't learned in training.

Inside the room, the three pig men had dropped their weapons as they desperately struggled to pull a fourth pig man out from under the rubble. Its legs were covered in rocks and debris. Trapped from the hips down, the creature flailed and squealed, desperate to wriggle free. The other three pig men didn't seem to be making much progress in freeing him.

Xander weighed his options, eyed their weapons, and looked down the hall. Surely, they would be busy long enough for him to get far from here. Their weapons looked old and primitive, but still better than his fists. He began to sneak towards the nearest sword when the creature under the rubble looked up and made eye contact with him.

He froze. He could run, but then all of this would have been for nothing. The three were unarmed, so if he could grab a weapon he could probably defeat them all. He tensed up and waited for the trapped pig man to give away his position, but it never happened.

It just stared into his eyes, whimpering in pain, but making no attempt to tell the others of the intruder. Marco relaxed a bit and looked back into its eyes and felt an instant understanding. This was no hardened warrior. It wasn't trained from birth to kill or be killed. This was just a creature doing what it had to do to survive. It didn't ask to be here any more than it asked to be trapped. Xander knew he hadn't caused the explosion, but somehow felt responsible anyway. He took a deep breath and stepped out of the shadows, hoping he was not making a fatal mistake.

As he stepped closer the three pig men spun around and scrambled for their weapons, grunting and oinking ferociously, but it didn't stop Xander. He slowly raised his hands, showing he was at their mercy, and pointed to the trapped creature. The pig men cautiously turned their heads to examine their trapped friend as it let out a slow, whimpering cry. The pig men all looked at each other, communicating in grunts and snorts. Then they finally lowered their weapons and stepped back, giving Xander room to fully assess the situation. He slowly approached the trapped pig man and extended his hand to show he was here to help. It snorted and made a face that Xander thought meant he was going to bite him. Instead, it winced in pain and lay down, doing what Xander could only assume was crying. He looked around and noticed that the rubble on top of it was made up of large heavy rocks and a solid wood beam with some of the wall still attached. He climbed up on the rubble, careful not to step on any part that was directly above the creature, and began to remove the large stones and toss them aside. One rolled after landing and fell into the newly created hole in the wall. He listened as it fell for what seemed like an eternity until he finally heard a small splash in the lava below. He shuddered to think of what might happen if he lost his balance. That was no way to go. Surprisingly, the other three creatures began to copy him, laying down their weapons once more and taking piece by piece off the pile. When most of the rocks were removed, one of the pig men jumped off the pile, took hold of the trapped pig man's arms, and began to pull, to the creature's immediate displeasure. It screamed. The offending pig man let go immediately and quickly looked up at Xander, sad desperation in its eyes. Xander jumped down and realized the issue. He pointed at two of the pig men and gestured to the large wooden post, signaling that they should lift it. They snorted in agreement and began to slowly lift the beam.

They grunted and strained under its weight. Xander knew they weren't going to last long. Should they slip, the trapped creature's life would be over. He gestured to the third pig man and pointed to one of the creature's arms as he grabbed the other and began to pull. It screamed, but nowhere near as loud as before, they were making progress! Xander and the other pig man kept pulling steadily, careful not to cause more damage by going too fast. The two holding the beam were struggling and one let out a squeal as the weight became too much. It slouched and the pillar came back down a few inches.

The injured pig man screamed, and Xander looked at the pig man next to him and nodded his head towards the pillar. It understood and ran to help the others without hesitation. With the extra help the beam was back up to where it had been, but barely. Xander pulled a bit more until suddenly the pig man's foot snagged on something. The beam proved to be too much for the three struggling pig men, and it began lowering once again, to everyone's horror. Xander, in a moment of desperation, dove into the hole in the rubble to see what was getting snagged.

The hoof of the pig man was stuck in some of the debris that had shifted. He worked to move the rocks as fast as he could, knowing that if the heavy beam came down now his quest, his very life, was over. When the last rock was moved, the creature pulled its leg out of the rocks. In an instant, Xander threw himself backward and out from under the pillar as it came crashing down, the dust shooting into his eyes and lungs. He lay on the floor, blind and coughing, fully expecting to see weapons pointed at him the second he regained his composure. What he saw instead shocked him.

The injured pig man was standing on one leg, using another pig man as support.

The remaining two were gathering the weapons, but clearly just to carry them, not to use them. Xander stood up, speechless. The injured pig man limped towards Xander and grabbed his wrist. His hand was filthy and covered in soot. The pig man slowly brought Xander's hand up and pressed his palm onto his pink face. He held Xander's hand there for a few moments and then let go. When Xander brought his hand back he saw a perfect black handprint on the pig man's face.

The creature nodded his head and made a sort of cooing noise, the other three followed suit. Xander understood he had earned this creature's, and by extension, this group's trust. Had he made allies in the depths of the Nether? Surely this could not be possible. He was taught that the creatures down here were bloodthirsty and animalistic. He shuddered to think about how different this whole situation would have played out had he still had his sword; had he approached with a more violent solution, or didn't stop when he had.

He bowed his head and attempted to make the cooing noise back, they immediately stopped. Had he offended them? He looked up and noticed they weren't even looking at him, they were looking… behind him?

He spun around to find a fifth pig man who seemed to have come out of nowhere. He tried cooing to him.

Bonk!

The pig man smacked Xander on the head with the handle of his sword and knocked him out. His body lay there utterly still for a few seconds before the pig man dragged him away.

Chapter 8: The Escape

"It is nobler to lay down and die for the Monarch than it is to betray any knowledge of Dragon Rock. For whatever pain and torment you may avoid will be delivered unto you tenfold in the great beyond."
- The Warrior's Code

"Squeeeeek"

Xander slowly regained consciousness. His vision was a little blurry, but it was clear enough that he was nowhere near where he had been knocked out. He groaned, and slowly sat up. He was in some sort of prison cell.

His eyes were slowly adjusting but weren't of much use to him now, with his limited view. He crossed his legs and closed his eyes, took a deep breath, and as he let it out he felt his perception grow and his understanding deepen. He was in a dungeon of some sort. He could feel the change in pressure, so he knew this was underground, but it wasn't as cold as he would expect, so he was sure he was not far under the lava sea. He could hear regular marching, most likely from the guard patrols.

He realized there weren't many of them. At first, he was relieved by this, but then he thought it was probably because escaping from here was too unlikely to warrant extra personnel. Many cells down he could hear voices, voices he could actually understand. More prisoners. One was a young boy, around his age from the sound of things. The other seemed to be a much older woman who spoke in rhymes.
This place gets weirder by the minute.

Slow, steady, and deliberate footsteps approached his cell. A guard was coming to check in on him. He didn't move. He continued to breathe and focus. He was focusing on the guard, his weapon, his stance, how tense he was. Did he have a key on him? Slowly a plan began to form in his mind. He could feign death on the guard's next round. He would play it up and make it seem like he was choking or in need of some sort of help. The guard seemed nervous, but not afraid of the inmates. No, he wanted to please his higher-ups.

The crudely made medals on his chest told a story all their own. Once he came close enough it would be no problem for Xander to incapacitate the guard, take his weapon and keys, double back to rescue the other prisoners and find a way out of there.

The guard stopped in front of Xander's cell, snorting and sniffing the air, trying to get an idea of what Xander was up to, but Xander wasn't focused on him anymore. He was focused on the quickly approaching footsteps, quiet but not invisible to his sense.

There were four traveling in a group, headed this way. The pig man guard noticed them, but too late. By the time he turned around they were practically on top of him. One of the group slammed the guard's head into the bars and, in one swift blow, rendered him unconscious, his body crumpling to the ground. They searched him and found a ring of keys. They went through a few of them in an attempt to open Xander's cell door. He was still sitting in his meditative state, far more comfortable relying on his warrior's sense than his naked eye. Their heart rates were fast. They knew they shouldn't be doing what they were doing, but they also felt that this was the right thing to do. The cell door swung open at last and one stepped in while the other three kept watch outside.

The visitor knelt before Xander and waited. Xander slowly opened his eyes and was face to face with a pig man, a pig man with a black handprint across its face. They locked eyes and the familiar bond and aura of understanding washed over Xander once more. The pig man was holding a stick and began drawing in the red sand on the floor of the cell. It drew a crude skull and looked up at Xander, pointing from the drawing to him, then drew a circle around the skull and a line stretching towards Xander.

Incredible, it knows why I'm here.

Xander nodded and the creature snorted in excitement. The creature then crossed out the skull with an X and looked saddened.

Does this mean there are no more?

The creature wiped away the drawing and this time traced a sword in the dirt, with another line going towards Xander.

"My people... killed them all?"

The creature snorted in agreement, this time noticeably less happy.

"That... can't be right. This is a time-honored tradition of my people. They hunted them all? When did this happen? I hadn't heard, so it must have been somewhat recently."

The creature wiped the drawings away yet again, redrawing the skull with an arrow stretching away from it.

"They've... been gone? That's impossible. Then what have all the warriors been bringing back as trophies?"

The creature locked eyes with Xander once again, in a slow, fluid motion, drags the stick across its own neck.

If Xander hadn't already been sitting, he would have been floored. He couldn't believe it. His tribe had been... cheating all these years, slaughtering these creatures that posed no real threat compared to the monsters they came after and passing off their accomplishment as an act of valor rather than murder.

He wanted to refuse this information, but he could tell this creature was being sincere or at least thought it was telling the truth. Honestly, this lined up perfectly with everything else he'd been finding out lately.

He took a deep breath.

So, if there are no wither skeletons, there is no need for me to be here.

He reached for the stick and the pig man obliged. He drew a crude portal in the sand and looked up at the creature. It stared at the picture, then looked up as if it were thinking. It suddenly snorted in excitement.

"Can you take me there?" Xander asked slowly.

The creature paused, then looked back at the other pig men, then back to Xander. It gestured to himself and the others. "You… Want to come with me?"

The creature snorted in a way that Xander understood as an affirmative with no room for negotiation. He weighed his options, before realizing he didn't really have a choice.

"Agreed."

The creature snorted and extended its hoof slowly towards Xander's face, softly pressing it there. They now each had each other's mark. They were brothers in battle. They had each saved one another's life and were now connected by an otherworldly bond. The two stood up to leave.

"What should I call you? Your name, what is it?"

The creature spewed an odd assortment of clicks and snorts. Xander just stared.

"Right. I'll never be able to repeat that. Mind if I just call you Hoglin?"

The creature seemed to laugh in approval.

Hoglin went over to the other pig men and told them something. They seemed to like it because they became very excited. Two of them dragged the unconscious guard into the cell while the third approached Xander. Hoglin was moved out of the cell and was now standing guard.

Xander tried to speak to the approaching pig man.

"Hey, do you think I could grab the guard's sword real quick –"

Before he could finish his sentence, the creature threw a cloth sack over his head and hoisted him over his shoulder. Nothing was working according to Xander's plans.

Chapter 9: The Struggle

"When in doubt, always follow the instinct that has been instilled in you. Trust your senses and training, second only to the word of your Monarch, for, without them, there would be no warrior"
- The Warrior's Code

The prison guard was knocked unconscious and Xander was sneaking out of the dungeon, so his whole plan wasn't completely up in smoke, but he had imagined knocking out the guard himself and walking out on his own two feet, not being carried over the shoulder of a pig man. Yet here he was. They were maneuvering the corridors expertly and without hesitation. Xander wondered if they were ever stationed down here on guard duty. Every once in a while, they would stop, questioned by a guard. Xander couldn't understand exactly what was being said but got the impression that Hoglin was a smooth grunter, for they were allowed to continue without a barrage of questions.

Since whatever was happening now was beyond his control, he allowed himself to get lost in thought. After all, he had a lot of information to process.

This whole experience was crazy. Were pig men really not as bad as he originally thought? Were his people in the past truly slaughtering these innocent pig men for no reason other than to cheat on their worthiness test? How long ago had the wither skeletons gone extinct? How many of his relatives and heroes actually cheated to get where they were now? How long would he have been down here before he decided to do the same thing?

I won't do that, not now that I know the truth. I have to expose this to the queen. Mother has to know what's been going on under her very nose.

He thought about Hoglin and the crew. They had seemed hostile at first but came to trust him over time. Were all the monsters like this? Or was it wrong to make generalizations about them? Maybe, like himself and his people, they each had different feelings and beliefs. He had known for some time that the monsters were smarter than he had first thought, but this was a life-changing experience. How many creatures had he slain stealthily, without giving them a chance? How many of those were just trying to eat and live? How many would have ignored him and his people? How many had he murdered?

"OOF!"

He had been slipping off the pig man's shoulder, who quickly and roughly adjusted him back in place, knocking the wind out of him.

Xander had almost no memory of his father. All he had were the larger-than-life stories he had grown up hearing. Xander himself imagined his father as some unstoppable, unwavering hero. He'd lost his father at a young age but now felt like he was losing him all over again. The heroic vision slowly crumbling at the realization that his great feats were nothing more than lies.

They stopped, and Xander was brought down and freed from the sack over his head. He wasn't ready for the brightness of the lava. They were back outside the fortress. He started to feel overwhelmed and frustrated at the thought of starting this journey all over again, but he looked at his new friends and felt a calm wash over him. At least this time, he wouldn't be alone.

"Hey guys, I want to thank you for getting me out of that tight spot back there, and for trusting me. I know my people have… hunted you in the past, but I intend to set things right. I promise you can trust me."

The pig men all nodded and snorted in agreement.

"Now, I know this is a really weird segue, but is there any way one of you could lend me a sword, so I don't feel so defense -"

Shoom, shoom, shoom…

Xander and the crew looked up quickly. A yellow-orange creature floating on top of two sets of rotating rods was flying down from the hole made in the fortress earlier

BOOM!

A fireball exploded between him and the pig men, creating a hole in the ground that crumbled away revealing lava underneath as smoke filled the area. It became near impossible to see and Xander started coughing. He took a few steps back and ran, jumping over the new hole to be on the same side as his Nether friends.

Shoom, shoom, shoom…

BOOM!

The Blaze fired at where Xander had been, the force of the explosion throwing him forward. He slammed into the edge and struggled to get his footing. He started to slip toward the hole when Hoglin dove forward, grabbing Xander's hand at the last second and pulling him to safety.

"We're gonna run out of places for handprints before long," Xander joked, but it was unclear if Hoglin understood what he meant or if he was just preoccupied. Hoglin and the rest of the pig men immediately took off running away from the blaze, with Xander not far behind.

Shoom, shoom, shoom…

BOOM!

Shoom, shoom, shoom…

BOOM!

Shoom, shoom, shoom…

BOOM!

Every time they got a few feet away another fireball threatened to close the gap, and each fireball was getting closer and closer. It wouldn't be long before the creature had adjusted its aim enough for a direct hit. He looked back to see how far the creature was. It was practically on top of them!

Shoom, shoom, shoom…

BOOM!

Hooves grabbed onto Xander, pulling him hard.

His distracted glance had caused him to miss the rest of them ducking into a narrow, hidden doorway, just in the nick of time. The fireball burst right above them, sealing them in.

He was checking himself for damage when Hoglin walked up and started tapping its hooves all over Xander as if making hoof prints. He had just saved his life multiple times from the blaze.

Xander laughed, "So, you did get it!"

Hoglin snorted and they all started down the only path available to them now.

They traveled in relative silence. One of the pig men was leading, followed by Xander and Hoglin, with the other two bringing up the rear. This suited Xander just fine because he had no idea where to go and was tired of asking for a weapon. After long hallways and twists and turns, they found themselves in a familiar-looking tunnel. It was nearly identical to the one at the cave. This was a ceremonial area. He slowly walked along the hallways, running his hand over the carvings of his people's history. The pictures show them fighting off dark creatures, killing gruesome beasts, and removing their skulls to the cheers of the village.

One of the images depicted a group of pig men being slaughtered. Xander looked down in shame, a single tear fighting its way free.

He wanted to apologize to Hoglin on his people's behalf but didn't know if he could find the words, or if it would do any good. He continued, looking at the twisted history of his people when he came to a pedestal. He didn't have any redstone torches this time, but this pedestal looked different. He turned around to ask the others what they thought he should do, but one of the pig men was already approaching, reaching into his bag. With a look of utter sadness on his face, he procured a skull and looked into its eye sockets longingly. He caressed the forehead and made a soft clicking sound.

The skull had belonged to someone he knew.

Slowly, gently, the pig man placed the skull upon the pedestal, and it instantly clicked and whirred. He took the skull and placed it back in his bag. The pedestal sank into the ground and two large hidden doors slid open, revealing a glowing purple portal, and two iron golem guards.

"We're going to have to find a way to get past them," Xander said.

When he heard no response, he looked behind him. The pig men were several steps back.

"Oh, come on guys, I don't even have a weapon!"

In a split second, every weapon they had been carrying was thrown in a pile at his feet.

"Alright then," Xander said, picking up a sword and crossbow. "Let's dance."

Chapter 10: The Golems

"Much like everything non-human, the golems are slow and dimwitted, but unlike the others, they have been molded to a purpose that suits us. Their usefulness alone sets them apart from the monsters."

- The Warrior's Code

Confidence swept through Xander's mind and took control of every muscle in his body.

"Hey, ugly!" Xander shouted.

The two iron golems stared straight ahead, ignoring his taunts completely.

"Come get some!" Xander yelled as he aimed his crossbow and fired an explosive bolt.

It hit one of the golems squarely in the face creating a small colorful explosion. He reloaded the crossbow as the smoke settled, aiming at the second golem when red eyes shone through the smoke, and with impossible speed, the golem moved to just inches in front of him. It hit him with its solid metal fist, sending him into the other golem, which shuddered awake on impact.

Great.

He scurried between the legs of the waking golem as it slammed its fist down where Xander had just been. Xander ran up the back of it, jumping off the head and over the other golem entirely. He ran back to the pile of weapons. His heart sank when he realized he hadn't thought this through very well, and none of these weapons would be useful against these ancient guards. Before he could formulate a new plan, the two were right by his side. He jumped out of the way as they each slammed their fists on the ground, destroying every weapon in the pile. He shot a glance over at his companions and made an apologetic face. One of them looked very upset at this loss.

He had to be careful. He was getting too close to Hoglin and the gang, and he wasn't sure he could get the golem's attention off of them and back onto himself if they noticed the pig men. The golems were in place, after all, to kill "monsters" on sight.

He lured the golems back to the portal room. Maybe if he could get behind the portal he could trick them into stepping through, then they could lose them back in his realm.

He ran towards the portal, but this simple action seemed to engage the golems, and they moved in faster than Xander could have imagined. In one fell swoop, a golem backhanded Xander into the other, who smacked him back to the room's entrance.

He lay on the ground, beaten and bloodied. How was he supposed to fight these two? It must have taken countless waves of creatures to destroy the two in the other cave.

And that's when it hit him. He had once again rushed into things without thinking, almost costing him his life as well as that of his new friends. He swore he would never make that mistake again. The golems slowly walked towards Xander, in no rush to get there quickly. He wasn't headed anywhere in his condition. Slowly, Xander began to drag himself towards the pig men, who began backing away in fear.

"S-stop... t-trust... me..." he managed to squeak out.

Hoglin ran forward and helped him up, allowing Xander to limp over to the others. The two golems, upon noticing the pig men, began to stomp forward a little bit faster, as if powered by bloodlust. Their red eyes glowed menacingly, their prime directive now squarely in front of them. With their massive frames, the two of them side by side took up the entire hallway. There would be no getting around them. Xander reached into one of the pig men's bag. It squealed and grabbed Xander's arm, but Hoglin placed a gentle hoof on its shoulder and clicked something softly. The pig man relinquished its grip. Xander pulled out the skull and turned to face the encroaching golems. Hoglin tried to help him walk, but Xander shooed Hoglin away and limped towards the behemoths unarmed and alone.

He held the skull in front of him and with shame dripping from his voice, said the words he'd been waiting to say his whole life.

"I, Prince Xander of Dragon Rock, have traveled to the Nether, land of monsters and unholy animals. I have done what needed to be done. I have…"

His voice caught in his throat and it was hard for him to swallow. But it was this, or die.

"I have found this foul beast and put it out of its misery with my trusty sword. Were it not for the need to return home and fight a nobler fight I would stay in this realm and slay them all, but they are worth neither the time nor the effort. So, I leave them for the next youngling and move on to greater conquests."

Xander was so full of shame he almost hoped it wouldn't work and the golems would end him then and there, but to his relief - and disappointment - they heard what they had been waiting to hear and saw the skull of the fallen. They slowly turned around and headed back to their spots, powered down and lifeless once more.

The pig men slowly approached Xander, understanding, but equally upset. Hoglin sobbed and wiped away tears. Xander tried to reach out but Hoglin ignored him and walked past.

I wonder if they even still want to come with me.

He held out the skull gently and tried to hand it back to the pig man he had borrowed it from, only to have it snatched back and shoved into the bag. Another pig man slammed his shoulder into Xander's on his way to the portal.

They all stepped through one by one, silently. Leaving Xander alone in the Nether to wonder if he was the monster after all.

Chapter 11: The Return

"When a fledgling warrior's quest is complete, it is then and only then that they are to be acknowledged as a warrior. They have earned the respect of their brethren, and villagers must show them the same courtesy they show the leaders of Dragon Rock. For without the warrior's offered protection, the villagers would be doomed."

- The Warrior's Code

Xander stepped through the portal last. He was dizzy and hazy, but he knew he was home. He appeared to be in some sort of temple. He had never been here before but recognized the Dragon Rock architecture. He stepped towards Hoglin and the others. They were huddled together, scared of the new atmosphere, the new sights, the new sounds. But mostly, terrified of their new "friend."

"I'm… I'm sorry guys. That was the only way, trust me. They were going to kill us."

He stopped. They weren't listening, either due to the sensory overload of taking in all the new sights and sounds, or the emotional overload of processing what they just saw Xander do. He understood this clearly and decided to get his bearings while they did the same.

The temple was made of white stone, and it was beautiful. Xander walked down the aisle leading to the only other thing in the room beside the portal, the door out.

I'll step outside and figure out where I am, the fresh air should do me good. Then, once Hoglin and the rest are ready to travel I'll take them home and explain everything.

Before he could get to the door, it flew open. Persephone walked in, accompanied by a small group of warriors.

"I thought I smelled rot and failure," she sneered.

Xander was not in the mood for this.

"Persephone, I demand you –"

"Oh, you're approaching me? Giving me demands? I had my suspicions, but this cinches it. Men, arrest the prince and the little monsters he brought with him. He is clearly not in the right state of mind."

He turned to run to his friends and defend them, to take them back through the portal and figure out another way. But it was too late. Before he got two steps in their direction he was tackled to the ground. He saw them huddled, scared as they were approached from all sides. As the guards closed in, Xander's world went black.

Water splashed on Xander's face, causing him to choke and wake up. He looked around. He was in another prison cell. This one was relatively nice, but a prison cell, nonetheless. Persephone was standing on the other side of the bars holding an empty bucket.

"Sorry for the confusion, my prince. You can never be too careful when those monsters are involved."

"Those monsters are my friends! Where are they?"

"Your friends? My, my, my, you must have been hit in the head harder than I thought. What a shame," she said in a sing-song voice. "I'd almost think you were under some sort of mind control if it weren't for the fact those savages are too dumb to think for themselves."

Xander knew it was pointless to argue. Persephone wasn't going to agree with him on the best of days, and she had been waiting for a moment like this for a year now.

"Yes, yes, you're right. Now can you please let me out of here so I can see my mother?"

"Right away, brave warrior." She leaned in. "You're lucky I had a platoon with me when I found you, or I'd have torn you to pieces and blamed it on your foul monster companions." She unlocked the cell door and stepped out of his way. "Make sure to wash up before you visit the queen. You have monster filth all over your face" He ignored her suggestion and marched straight to the throne room. Forgoing all diplomacy, he slammed open the palace doors, to the guards' dismay, and marched straight towards his mother.

"Xander! My son, I'm so glad to see you!" Athena immediately rose from her chair and greeted her son with a big smile.

"Please tell me you have it."

He looked at her dumbfounded. "Have what?"

"The skull, my son. What else?" Xander shook himself out of his stupor, how could he have forgotten? "You did pass the test, did you not?"

"Mother, you don't understand."

At this, the throne room doors were thrown open once again.

"ARE YOU KIDDING ME?" shouted the guard in charge of the doors. He mumbled something under his breath and proceeded to close them... again.

Persephone marched down the aisle towards the queen.

What is she up to?

"Not only did young Xander pass, my lady, but he passed with flying colors. He brought the skull back alright." As she said this, she held the skull of a pig man up in the air, the skull his pig man companion had guarded with his life.

"Where are they?" Xander roared.

"Xander, what has gotten into you? Persephone was talking. Please, go on."

"Thank you, my queen. As I was saying, he passed with flying colors. He did something that has never been done in our long and storied history. He brought four live specimens back with him for the rest of our people to enjoy!"

Xander was filled with a rage he had never known before.

"NO!" he screamed, then turned to the queen.

"Mother, you don't understand. I didn't, I brought back friends, creatures that helped me on my journey. These pig men, they aren't our enemies. They can be worked with, reasoned with. They aren't the monsters you think they are! And furthermore, this whole military is built on lies! The warriors who go into the Nether are killing pig men, not wither skeletons. They aren't fighting for their lives to prove anything. They follow a laid-out path. They kill the first innocent creature they see and pop on back! They're all murderers! Wither skulls don't even exist anymore!"

The queen was taken aback by the outburst. After a moment, she regained her composure and turned to Persephone.

"Persephone, what is the meaning of this?"

"Apologies, my queen."

Xander was beside himself. He was going to save his friends and change the way things were done around there. Watching Persephone get in trouble would just be icing on the cake.

"Am I to understand you sent my boy down into the depths thinking he was looking for a wither skeleton? How did you leave out so much of our history and traditions? What if he was hurt down there?"

Xander felt his stomach churn. He was going to be sick. How could his mother have known and been ok with all this?

Persephone shot him a sly, knowing smile.

"With all due respect, you know how Xander can be. I tried to inform him, but he simply ignored me during the whole journey to the cave. I think he still feels great guilt for what happened a year ago. I've expressed my forgiveness for him, but he's just too hard on himself."

"On that, we can agree, Persephone."

Xander couldn't believe his ears. Everyone knew but him. That didn't seem right. Persephone sent him into the Nether to die? That… was pretty on-brand. The queen's advisor stepped out of the shadows and walked past the queen, directly to Persephone, and whispered something in her ear, before returning to her usual spot.

The queen looked perplexed. "What is the meaning of this? Why is my advisor speaking directly to you?"

"My apologies," Persephone bowed. "I had a surprise. I was hoping I could reveal it to you myself when the time was right. She was simply informing me that time was now. I hope you don't mind, but I set up a little extra celebration. Before Xander officially becomes a warrior, we will all head to the village square. For the first time in ages, we're going to have a good old fashioned monster execution."

Xander's blood ran cold.

Chapter 12: The Execution

"There is no greater pleasure to be had than sharing the joys of monster slaughter with those unworthy of taking part in it personally"
- The Warrior's Code

The crowd was lively and the words "pig men" and "Nether" rumbled throughout the town.

An electrical excitement filled the air and made Xander sick to his stomach.

"How could a pig man even get here? I thought all the portals were guarded?" a citizen asked.

"This is perfect weather for a little monster-slaying, wouldn't you think?" another said to his children.

The crowd started getting loud and cheering.

From up on stage, Xander sat next to his mother. He felt helpless now but knew that when the time came, this would be the best place to be. Now, if only he could come up with a plan. The town crowded before him, excited in equal parts for Xander's victory and the entertaining bloodshed.

The things people were saying were making his blood boil, but he couldn't help but wonder if he'd be echoing these same sentiments had this happened before he had met Hoglin and the crew.

Persephone took center stage and the crowd quieted.

"Fellow citizens of Dragon Rock, our reason for gathering here today is twofold but will serve us all the same. It will bring us together and begin a new chapter in our lives. Today, we are celebrating Xander's final achievement. He traveled down deep into the Nether, the very den of evil itself, and he defeated a *wither skeleton.*"

Her inflection and the subsequent laugh rippling through the crowd made Xander question everything once again. Did *everyone* know there were no more wither skeletons?

"But that wasn't enough for our bravest and brightest, oh no. He saw fit to bring us all a gift. Not wanting to hog, pardon the pun, his glory all to himself, he was kind enough to bring four of the beasts back with him, so that we might all feel like warriors today!"

At the mention of the pig men, four guards marched out Hoglin and the crew, their mouths gagged. Pure, abject horror was in their eyes. Seeing them like this filled Xander with disgust. They were all brought to the back of the stage. One-by-one a noose was placed around each of their necks. Hoglin was the last to get fitted. He looked over towards Xander, pleading with his eyes, but was promptly punched in the stomach by a guard.

"Don't you dare lay eyes on our royalty, you foul beast," he spat while putting the noose in place.

"Now that I've bored you enough with my speech, how about a little public execution, by the hands of our newest warrior?"

The crowd went wild as Xander's heart sank to the floor. He was not expecting this, though, knowing Persephone, he really should have been. He stood slowly, looking over at his mom who was beaming and clapping along with the crowd. He walked towards Persephone, who was casually leaning on the lever that would send his friends to oblivion. Persephone patted him on the back, then leaned in.

"My friends died by your hands. Now your friends get to suffer the same fate. Then we'll be even, little warrior."

He gulped. He was stuck. He couldn't execute his friends, but he couldn't see a way out of this mess with all of them still alive. So, he decided not to "see," but instead to rely on the senses that had saved him time and time again. He placed his hand on the lever, closed his eyes, and took a deep breath. The world around him fell silent once more.

He was on a raised stage, to his right was a guard making sure the staircase wasn't rushed by excited civilians. To his left, the gallows with his four friends. In front of the stage was a roped-off section for the horses of the guards that were patrolling the crowd. He looked behind him. His mother was sitting on her throne, looking proud as can be, with Persephone and the advisor on either side of her.

Persephone looked happier than she had been the day Dulan proposed.

He looked out to the crowd. These people he had known his whole life seemed like strangers at this moment. They were hooting and hollering, their unquenchable bloodlust made vocal. Xander had fought his whole life to be given the honor to defend them, and now he wanted nothing more than to be far, far away from them. The queen nodded at Xander. She was ready for the show. Xander planned on giving them a show, alright. He gripped the lever and pulled it as hard as he could.

...the opposite way. Instead of releasing the trapdoors, the lever snapped right off, rendering the gallows useless. But more importantly, it finally gave Xander a weapon. The guard watching the stairs looked shocked.

"Oops, looks like you pulled it too hard the wrong way, my lord." he said as he began walking towards Xander, "Not to worry, that's not the first time it's happened. Here, let's get you fixed –"

WHACK!

Xander took the handle and smashed the guard in the face as hard as he could, instantly knocking him out. He threw the lever at the guard running towards him from across the stage. He bent down and pulled the sword out of the unconscious guard's sheath. Several guards had made it through the crowd and began running up the stairs to grab Xander, but he was one step ahead of them. He kicked the large, limp guard and sent him rolling down the stairs knocking the pursuing guards back down the stairs. The crowd gasped as Xander took the sword and cut the rope that all the nooses were connected to, setting the pig men free.

At the realization that the "monsters" were now loose, the crowd began screaming and running away, trampling each other in an attempt to get to safety. Xander jumped off the stage and onto one of the stationed guard's horses. He turned around to face his mom as the pig men followed his lead, all leaping from the stage and mounting horses of their own.

"I'm sorry, mother, but this is how it needs to be. If you truly would have let these innocent be creatures murdered in cold blood for entertainment, then I fully renounce my title and my citizenship."

The queen shouted back over the crowd to Xander.

"You don't have to do this, Xander. You don't have to throw your life away for these monsters!"

"I'm not. You're the only monsters I see here. So, I'm taking my new people far away from the likes of you."

Queen Athena was angrier than he had ever seen her, but that was nothing compared to Persephone.

"KILL THE BEASTS AND BRING ME THE BOY!" she screamed, but it was too late. Xander and the pig men reared back on their stolen horses, jumped the fence, and galloped through what little of the crowd remained. They rode as hard and as fast as they could. Everyone seemed to be on the same page without a word between them.

They rode to the temple and dismounted the horses, shooing them off into the wild. They busted through the doors and dove through the portal, taking their chances with the Nether rather than the angry mob. As soon as they were in the Nether, they took off running, past the golems who wouldn't chase them far. They were much more concerned with things attempting to escape from the Nether than anything entering. Hoglin took the lead and they made their way to a safe room deep in the nether fortress. They stayed here, catching their breath, and trying to figure out what to do next.

Epilogue

"The kingdom was forged by dragon's fire, and the beast was gone as quickly as it appeared. But one day, when it returns, all the world will be Dragon Rock."
- The Warrior's Code

The queen was furious. Her son was gone, and her people were restless. This did not bode well. She feared history may repeat itself. She stopped the guards in their pursuit. Her son was dead to her, and she didn't want to waste resources on a traitor. Instead, she wanted them here, policing the streets, squashing any form of rebellion or infighting.

She stormed back to her palace, flanked by Persephone and Apophis. She was about to enter when the ground began to shake violently. The villagers ran about in a panic. To them, it felt like the world was ending. The palace began to crumble and implode upon itself. The three women just watched and waited. When the shaking ended and the smoke was settled, a large portal lay where the palace once stood. Slowly, a figure rose out of it. It was a man, a completely ordinary man but for his glowing, deep purple eyes. He walked forward. The queen came to meet him.

"Were you successful, my love?" She asked.

"But, of course." He smiled. "Where is my son?"

"I'm afraid he's gone. He chose to side with weaklings. He has no place in our society."

"So be it," the warrior king said emotionlessly. "It's time for Dragon Rock to once again claim its name and this land."

The roar of a great beast echoed up from the portal.

The End.

PS.

Just wanted to take this time to thank you for your continued support. Please know that all of this is not possible without you!

If you want to be a part of our Hall of Fame, please drop us a rating and let us know who your favorite characters are, what we can improve on, or any suggestions at all.
Thank you again!

From,

Mr. Crafty

Crafty Universe
Hall of Fame

Alayna A   Joyce Z   Jeff Jasper   M. heckscher

Mary J Bailey   Lizzie Greene   Samantha D.

Cj-2007   tonylihan   MrPerson2econd   Taghreed

Sheridy Mouton   Serge   Lianne McKee

Laura M. Busse   Jessica Ermie   Jennifer Caffelle

Hugh A Hoebbel   Frank Barrios   Alayna A

www.ingramcontent.com/pod-product-compliance
Lightning Source LLC
Chambersburg PA
CBHW020504030426
42337CB00011B/222